T0082781

Kids' 50 days Prompt Journal

Encouraging your kids to write a short stories

FEERA FIRZA

PARTRIDGE

Copyright © 2021 by Feera Firza.

ISBN: Softcover   978-1-5437-6418-5
               eBook   978-1-5437-6419-2

All rights reserved. No part of this book may be used or reproduced by any means, graphic, electronic, or mechanical, including photocopying, recording, taping or by any information storage retrieval system without the written permission of the author except in the case of brief quotations embodied in critical articles and reviews.

Because of the dynamic nature of the Internet, any web addresses or links contained in this book may have changed since publication and may no longer be valid. The views expressed in this work are solely those of the author and do not necessarily reflect the views of the publisher, and the publisher hereby disclaims any responsibility for them.

Print information available on the last page.

To order additional copies of this book, contact
Toll Free +65 3165 7531 (Singapore)
Toll Free +60 3 3099 4412 (Malaysia)
orders.singapore@partridgepublishing.com

www.partridgepublishing.com/singapore

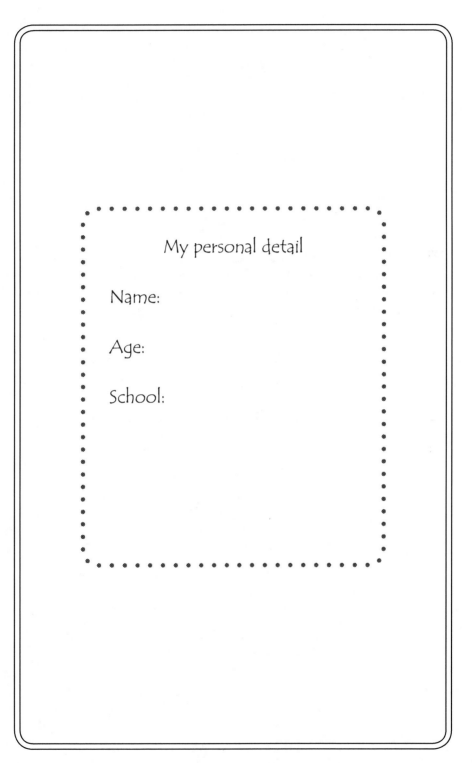

My personal detail

Name:

Age:

School:

Date:

Prompt story #1

Write a story about an enchanted forest. What would you will be in your enchanted story?

_____

_____

_____

_____

_____

_____

_____

_____

_____

_____

_____

_____

_____

_____

_____

_____

_____

Date:

Prompt story #2

Who is your favorite superhero? Tell a story about your
superhero.

_____

_____

_____

_____

_____

_____

_____

_____

_____

_____

_____

_____

_____

_____

_____

_____

Date:

Prompt story #3

What is your favorite season? Tell a story about your
experience during that season.

_____

_____

_____

_____

_____

_____

_____

_____

_____

_____

_____

_____

_____

_____

_____

_____

_____

_____

Date:

Prompt story #4

Write a story about your mother or father.

_____

_____

_____

_____

_____

_____

_____

_____

_____

_____

_____

_____

_____

_____

_____

_____

_____

_____

_____

Date:

Prompt story #5

If you had super powers, what would they be? Write about the advantages and disadvantages of this superpower.

_____

_____

_____

_____

_____

_____

_____

_____

_____

_____

_____

_____

_____

_____

_____

_____

_____

Date:

Prompt story #6

Create a story using these word (rainbow, sun, rain, cloudy).

_____

_____

_____

_____

_____

_____

_____

_____

_____

_____

_____

_____

_____

_____

_____

_____

_____

_____

_____

_____

Date:

Prompt story #7

While walking on a corridor, you come across a 100 dollar
note. What would you do with this money?

_____

_____

_____

_____

_____

_____

_____

_____

_____

_____

_____

_____

_____

_____

_____

_____

Date:

Prompt story #8

Describe a holiday with your family? What was interesting about this holiday?

_____

_____

_____

_____

_____

_____

_____

_____

_____

_____

_____

_____

_____

_____

_____

_____

_____

Date:

Prompt story #9

What would you do if you woke up one morning to find yourself in the middle of a vast sea, with a dolphin by your side?

_____

_____

_____

_____

_____

_____

_____

_____

_____

_____

_____

_____

_____

_____

_____

_____

Date:

Prompt story #10

If you were given a chance to be the moon or the sun, which one would you be? Why?

_____

_____

_____

_____

_____

_____

_____

_____

_____

_____

_____

_____

_____

_____

_____

_____

Date:

Prompt story #11

Write a story about something unforgettable in your life.

_____

_____

_____

_____

_____

_____

_____

_____

_____

_____

_____

_____

_____

_____

_____

_____

_____

_____

Date:

Prompt story #12

If you were given a chance to be a Disney character, which character would you choose? Tell a story about your chosen character.

_____

_____

_____

_____

_____

_____

_____

_____

_____

_____

_____

_____

_____

_____

_____

_____

Date:

Prompt story #13

Who is your favourite Disney princess? Tell a story about your favourite princess.

_____

_____

_____

_____

_____

_____

_____

_____

_____

_____

_____

_____

_____

_____

_____

_____

_____

Date:

Prompt story #14

If you could spend a day with Disney princess, what are the activities you do together.

_____

_____

_____

_____

_____

_____

_____

_____

_____

_____

_____

_____

_____

_____

_____

_____

_____

Date:

Prompt story #15

If you were given a chance to meet a dinosaur, which dinosaur would you meet? Describe the dinosaur.

_____

_____

_____

_____

_____

_____

_____

_____

_____

_____

_____

_____

_____

_____

_____

_____

_____

_____

Date:

Prompt story #16

If you parents gave you some pocket money and gave you permission to get your favorite toy. What toy would you choose? Describe your toy.

_____

_____

_____

_____

_____

_____

_____

_____

_____

_____

_____

_____

_____

_____

_____

Date:

Prompt story #17

If you were given a chance to help people who are in trouble, what would you do to make their life better?

_____

_____

_____

_____

_____

_____

_____

_____

_____

_____

_____

_____

_____

_____

_____

_____

Date:

Prompt story #18

Describe your first day at school. What did you like or dislike about this experience?

_____

_____

_____

_____

_____

_____

_____

_____

_____

_____

_____

_____

_____

_____

_____

_____

_____

Date:

Prompt story #19

Who is your best friend at school? Describe your friend's good qualities and the activities you do together.

_____

_____

_____

_____

_____

_____

_____

_____

_____

_____

_____

_____

_____

_____

_____

_____

_____

Date:

Prompt story #20

Which country would you choose for a holiday with your family? Why would you choose this country?

_____

_____

_____

_____

_____

_____

_____

_____

_____

_____

_____

_____

_____

_____

_____

_____

_____

_____

Date:

Prompt story #21

Describe your favourite food. How do you prepare your favourite food?

_____

_____

_____

_____

_____

_____

_____

_____

_____

_____

_____

_____

_____

_____

_____

Date:

Prompt story #22

Do you have a pet? If you do, describe your experience with your pet, from the day you first met it. If you do not, then, what pet would you like to have, and, why?

_____

_____

_____

_____

_____

_____

_____

_____

_____

_____

_____

_____

_____

_____

_____

_____

Date:

Prompt story #23

If you are given a chance to choose a planet to live on, other than earth, which planet would it be, and, why?

_____

_____

_____

_____

_____

_____

_____

_____

_____

_____

_____

_____

_____

_____

_____

_____

_____

Date:

Prompt story #24

Describe your country. What would you tell your pen pal about your country?

_____

_____

_____

_____

_____

_____

_____

_____

_____

_____

_____

_____

_____

_____

_____

_____

Date:

Prompt story #25

Create a story based on these word, (river/bird/jungle/ hungry and fruits)

_____

_____

_____

_____

_____

_____

_____

_____

_____

_____

_____

_____

_____

_____

_____

_____

Date:

Prompt story #26

What is your ambition? Why did you choose this ambition?

_____

_____

_____

_____

_____

_____

_____

_____

_____

_____

_____

_____

_____

_____

_____

_____

_____

_____

_____

Date:

Prompt story #27

Describe your dream house and the things you would like to have in it.

_____

_____

_____

_____

_____

_____

_____

_____

_____

_____

_____

_____

_____

_____

_____

_____

_____

Date:

Prompt story #28

Describe your hobby. Why did you choose this hobby and when did you start it?

_____

_____

_____

_____

_____

_____

_____

_____

_____

_____

_____

_____

_____

_____

_____

Date:

Prompt story #29

Describe your favourite book. Why do you love this book?

_____

_____

_____

_____

_____

_____

_____

_____

_____

_____

_____

_____

_____

_____

_____

_____

_____

_____

_____

Date:

Prompt story #30

If you were a film director, what sort of a film would you direct?

_____

_____

_____

_____

_____

_____

_____

_____

_____

_____

_____

_____

_____

_____

_____

_____

_____

_____

Date:

Prompt story #31

If you were given a chance to change the ending of a Disney story, which one of it would you choose, and, how would you end it?

_____

_____

_____

_____

_____

_____

_____

_____

_____

_____

_____

_____

_____

_____

_____

_____

Date:

Prompt story #32

What is your name? If you were given the chance to choose your own name, what would you name yourself, and, why?

_____

_____

_____

_____

_____

_____

_____

_____

_____

_____

_____

_____

_____

_____

_____

_____

_____

_____

Date:

Prompt story #33

Describe your neighbourhood. What is the best thing about your neighbourhood?

_____

_____

_____

_____

_____

_____

_____

_____

_____

_____

_____

_____

_____

_____

_____

_____

_____

_____

Date:

Prompt story #34

What is it that you most like about yourself? Describe
yourself.

_____

_____

_____

_____

_____

_____

_____

_____

_____

_____

_____

_____

_____

_____

_____

_____

_____

Date:

Prompt story #35

Share your experience about celebrating any festival in your country.

_____

_____

_____

_____

_____

_____

_____

_____

_____

_____

_____

_____

_____

_____

_____

_____

_____

Date:

Prompt story #36

What is your favourite cartoon show? Describe your favourite cartoon show.

_____

_____

_____

_____

_____

_____

_____

_____

_____

_____

_____

_____

_____

_____

_____

_____

_____

Date:

Prompt story #37

Which character would you choose to be in the Kung Fu Panda movie (po/tigress/mantis/crane or viper)? Why would you choose to be this character?

_____

_____

_____

_____

_____

_____

_____

_____

_____

_____

_____

_____

_____

_____

_____

_____

Date:

Prompt story #38

If you were given an item that you could recycle, for example, paper, plastic or glass, what would you do?

_____

_____

_____

_____

_____

_____

_____

_____

_____

_____

_____

_____

_____

_____

_____

_____

Date:

Prompt story #39

Which is your favourite Tom & Jerry cartoon character,
and, why?

_____

_____

_____

_____

_____

_____

_____

_____

_____

_____

_____

_____

_____

_____

_____

_____

_____

Date:

Prompt story #40

If you were given the chance to go on an adventure, what kind of an adventure would you choose?

_____

_____

_____

_____

_____

_____

_____

_____

_____

_____

_____

_____

_____

_____

_____

_____

_____

Date:

Prompt story #41

What are your family's summer activities? Describe these activities that you do with your family.

_____

_____

_____

_____

_____

_____

_____

_____

_____

_____

_____

_____

_____

_____

_____

_____

_____

_____

Date:

Prompt story #42

What is your favourite traditional costume, and, why?

_____

_____

_____

_____

_____

_____

_____

_____

_____

_____

_____

_____

_____

_____

_____

_____

_____

_____

Date:

Prompt story #43

What is your favourite sport, and, why?

_____

_____

_____

_____

_____

_____

_____

_____

_____

_____

_____

_____

_____

_____

_____

_____

_____

Date:

Prompt story #44

If you were given a chance to choose between the characters of a pirate and a princess, which would you choose, and, why?

_____

_____

_____

_____

_____

_____

_____

_____

_____

_____

_____

_____

_____

_____

_____

_____

Date:

Prompt story #45

If you were given an art paper, what would you draw, and, why?

_____

_____

_____

_____

_____

_____

_____

_____

_____

_____

_____

_____

_____

_____

_____

_____

Date:

Prompt story #46

Imagine yourself as a watch. Describe your life as a watch.

_____

_____

_____

_____

_____

_____

_____

_____

_____

_____

_____

_____

_____

_____

_____

_____

_____

_____

Date:

Prompt story #47

If you were a Disney princess, what kind of a character would you have? (for examples: brave, kind, bold, intelligent and others)

_____

_____

_____

_____

_____

_____

_____

_____

_____

_____

_____

_____

_____

_____

_____

_____

Date:

Prompt story #48

Which is your favourite Harry Potter character? Why do you like this character?

_____

_____

_____

_____

_____

_____

_____

_____

_____

_____

_____

_____

_____

_____

_____

_____

_____

Date:

Prompt story #49

If you were given the chance to change the ending of the Lion King movie, how would you end it?

_____

_____

_____

_____

_____

_____

_____

_____

_____

_____

_____

_____

_____

_____

_____

Date:

Prompt story #50

Write a story about your favourite idol.

_____

_____

_____

_____

_____

_____

_____

_____

_____

_____

_____

_____

_____

_____

_____

_____

_____

_____

_____

_____

Printed in the United States
by Baker & Taylor Publisher Services